# LIFE IN THE SONORAN DESERT

# BOOK TWO

## By Robert Frieders, Ph. D.

### A Yankoo Desert  Series Book

**COVER:** The humming bird has a long tongue.  It extends the tongue into the flower until it reaches the nectar pool at the base of the flower.  Then it draws up the liquid nectar through a hollow tube in its tongue. This drinking process is similar to a human " using a straw" to drink liquids.

*Photo by Earle A. Robinson*

**Yankoo Publishing Co.**

# LIFE IN THE SONORAN DESERT

## BOOK TWO

### By Robert Frieders, Ph.D.

All photographs and line drawings by the author unless indicated otherwise.

Published by: The Yankoo Publishing Co.
10616 W. Cameo Drive
Sun City, Az 85351-2708

Copyright 2005          by Robert Frieders

First Printing 2005

Printed in the United States of America

Library of Congress Catalog Card Number: 98-61677

ISBN 0-9639284-7-3

# Acknowledgments

I wish to thank my wife, Dottie, and all our friends who have helped make this book a reality.

Dr. Mamie Ross, Consultant
Mrs. Shirley Oshinski, Editor

We are also grateful to the following who have allowed us to use their photos of the Sonoran Desert animals for this book.

Earle A. Robinson
George Olin
Arizona Game and Fish Dept.
Greg Clark

We are grateful to our many readers who have been so complimentary on both, Book One on the Sonoran Desert and the series of books on the Oak Hickory Forest. Come travel with Ranger Roscoe as the "Friend." He will guide you through our desert. In your travels, you will see many desert plants and animals. You will learn how they live in our desert. One gains a greater knowledge and appreciation of these animals and plants living in the Sonoran Desert. ***ENYOY YOUR TRIP THROUGH OUR DESERT!***

# TABLE OF CONTENTS

# CHAPTER ONE
# RANGER ROSCOE AND THE ROADRUNNER

Hello, my Friend! Do you remember me? I'm R a n g e r Roscoe, the American elf who guided you in the first desert book. Let's travel together again through the S o n o r a n Desert.

We, elves, will tell you more about our interesting and wonderful desert plants and animals.

Let's be on our way!

Photo by Earle A. Robinson

Look at that Roadrunner, my Friend! That bird can be found all year in our desert. It does not migrate out during the hot, dry season like some desert birds. The Roadrunner is a solitary bird. One does not see groups of Roadrunners. One can often see the Roadrunner darting in and out between the desert trees and shrubs. It is unlike other birds. It spends most of the time moving on the ground. It only flies when frightened. Sometimes, it will glide downhill. Notice. The body of the Roadrunner is rather compact. The bird has a long tail. It is as long as its body.

 The bird has a large bill. The bill is hooked at the tip.

When excited the bird erects a feather crest on its head. At other times the crest is laid back on the head. The Roadrunner has long strong legs.
Two toes face forward.
Two toes face backward.

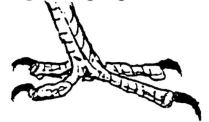

Looking at a  Roadrunner's tracks, it's difficult to determine in which direction the bird is moving.

The Roadrunner is a fast runner. It can swiftly dodge in and around desert vegetation.  It can take many steps per second.  It can out run both the  coyote and the fox.  The Roadrunner can also make some rather long jumps.

When running fast, its long neck is pointed straight out front.  Its short wings are outstretched.  These stubby wings move slightly up and down when running. Also, when running,  the tail moves up and down.

It appears that both the wing and tail movements increase the Roadrunner's speed. In running fast, it can stop quickly. To brake, the bird expands its tail feathers into a fan. It pulls this fan tail up toward the head in braking.

The bird can also turn in an instant. It can swerve from one side to the other, going one way and then another way. If the tail swings to the right, the bird's body goes to the left. Off it goes in that direction!

If the tail swings to the left, the bird's body heads toward the right. Off it goes in that direction! The tail acts as a rudder. It makes possible the bird's great maneuverability.

The Roadrunner makes its nest in cactus, small trees, or taller bushes. The nest is a tangle of twigs. The birds take turns warming the eggs in the nest. When not on the nest, the birds forage for food.

Look here at this Roadrunner's nest!

Photo by Earle A. Robinson

It is in a Cholla cactus. The nest is filled with young. You can see that some have just hatched from the eggs.

Roadrunners catch and feed on many kinds of animals. Snakes, lizards, rats, mice, insects, horned toads, snails, cactus fruits and berries all serve as food for a Roadrunner. They chase and capture lizards. They swallow the lizard head first.

The Roadrunner can kill a rattlesnake. The bird is very agile. It strikes the snake with its beak. The strike with its bill is quicker than the snake's reaction. Its beak pounds the snake's body against the ground. It will kill the snake in this way.

The Roadrunner swallows all animals head first. Snakes, being a long food, at times, prove to be a problem. The Roadrunner swallows most of the snake. But it runs out of room inside its body for the whole meal. So part of the snake is left hanging outside the mouth.

There is no room for it now. This doesn't seem to hinder the Roadrunner's movements. It carries on with the snake dangling from its mouth. As the food in the stomach is digested, room will be made. Then the last part of the snake will disappear.

Look at that rattlesnake over there in the sand! That is a Sidewinder Rattlesnake!

Photo by Earle A. Robinson

It was named the "Sidewinder Rattlesnake" because it travels sidewise on the sandy desert surface.

Observe this close-up picture of the Sidewinder Rattlesnake's head.  See the hornlike projection over each eye.

Photo by George Olin

The Sidewinder Rattlesnake is a pit viper.  It is a small snake.  It grows to twenty or thirty inches long. During the day it remains buried in the sand beneath the shade of a bush or tree.  At night, it comes out to forage for food.  The Sidewinder will capture and eat Kangaroo Rats, lizards, and mice.There goes that Sidewinder Rattlesnake! Look at the trail it leaves.

# CHAPTER TWO

## THE OCOTILLO and THE GECKO

My Friend, look at that plant.
That is an Ocotillo. It is also
called "Coach Whip."
It has the shape of a funnel.
The clump of long slender
stems are attached to one
another near the ground.
The stems can be up to
fifteen feet long. They do
not branch. Each stem is
covered with thorny
projections. These thorns led
to another name, "Cat's Claw."

This shrub is leafless during most of the year. When it rains, leaves quickly appear. A number of leaves arise where each thorn comes off the stem.
These leaves remain as long as there is sufficient water. As a dry season begins, the leaves turn brown and are shed. Again the long stems are leafless. Leaves can be produced and dropped a number of times during a year.

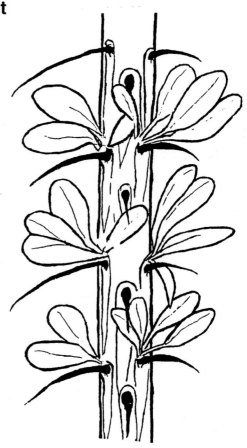

In dry times, the leafless stems now do what leaves do in wet times. They become green in color and carry on photosynthesis.

"Photosynthesis" means "putting together with light." Let me explain this process. All green plants have green pigment. This makes leaves and stems green. The green pigments in plant structures receive energy from the sun's rays.

The green structures are like factories. They take water and carbon dioxide and make building blocks. Some blocks are arranged as leaves. Others are arranged as stems, roots, flowers, or seeds. This is photosynthesis! Green plant structures, using the energy of the sun's rays, construct building blocks from water and carbon dioxide.

Below the inner bark of the stem is a layer of resin cells. These cells reduce water loss from the stem to the dry air. During dry periods, one can cut off a section of the stem. If one lights the cut end with a match, it will burn. This has led to another name for this shrub.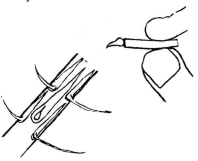
It is sometimes called "Candlewood."

Here red flower clusters can be seen on the ends of these stems in May and June. The petals of these flowers are united, lengthwise, forming a floral tube.

Humming birds put their long tube-like tongue into the nectar pools. The tongue functions like a straw. Nectar in tubular flowers is a favorite food of the Hummingbirds.

There's Ebenezer, my Friend. Let's go over and see what he is looking at! Hi, Ebenezer! Hi, Ranger Roscoe! Look what we have here. There are some small lizards. They are small Geckos.

Photo by George Olin

Notice the brownish, black bands evident on the body and tail. The skin is tan colored. It is not covered with scales. The skin of most lizards has scales. Notice the lizards' large protruding eyes. Those eyes are excellent for night vision. The Gecko has short legs. Each leg ends in slender toes that are clawed. The Gecko hides during the day.

The Gecko is found in shallow burrows or under rocks or desert debris. At night it comes out seeking food. The Gecko feeds on insects and spiders. It twitches its tail as it stalks an animal. Once close to the prey, it flips out a long tongue. It grabs the prey with its tongue and swallows it.

The Kit Fox and other animals search for Geckos. When a predator is about to grasp it, the Gecko can break off part of its tail.

The discarded tail piece jumps back and forth. The surprised predator watches this motion of the active tail piece. This gives the Gecko time to

scurry away. The Gecko is now safe. It will generate a new tail. There goes that Gecko! Well, I must get busy looking for other lizards. Good bye, Roscoe and friend.

Goodbye, Ebenezer!

# CHAPTER THREE

## THE SCORPION AND THE SOW BUG

**Look at that animal, my Friend.  It is a scorpion.**

Photo by George Olin

**Scorpions are rather small animals.  The largest scorpions are only about five inches long. Notice the large lobster-like pincers on that scorpion.**

**There are two eyes in the center of its head. Scorpions have three to five additional eyes on each side of the head.**

**It has four walking legs on each side.**

A scorpion has a small mouth.  Near the mouth are two hand-like structures.

The tail end of the scorpion is made up of segments. One can see these segments on that scorpion. It has twelve such segments.

The last five tail segments curl upwards toward the head.

The last segment ends in a needle-like stinger. Inside this segment is a poison gland. A muscle around this gland will force poison out of the gland up a hollow tube to the stinger. The hollow stinger has an opening near its needle-like end. The scorpion can force the poison through the needle into the body of the prey animal.

Scorpions are active at night.  During the day they stay under rocks, desert debris, or in crevices in the ground.

At night the scorpions head out for food. Spiders, insects, and small animals are scorpion food. A scorpion detects prey by the sound of sand movements a prey makes. This directs the scorpion toward an animal. Then the scorpion stops. When the prey moves again, the scorpion moves closer. The scorpion grabs the animal with its large pincers. That curled-up tail moves over the scorpion's body. It plunges the needle stinger into the prey. Poison from the gland shoots into the prey. The poison kills the animal.

The large pincers then move the prey to the mouth. There two strong hand-like structures grab it. The scorpion bites into the animal. Digestive juices are shot into the wound. These juices break down the prey's body parts into a liquid solution. Then the scorpion sucks this liquid out of the prey. When it has finished, only the outer shell remains.

Scorpions protect themselves from predators by hiding during the day. Scorpions are vulnerable when they search for food. Many night animals also eat scorpions. Owls, snakes, Kit Fox, and rodents all eat scorpions.

Female scorpions give birth to live young. The young look like miniature adults. The young scorpions ride on the female's back until they shed their skin the first time. Now a new larger skin will cover the animal.

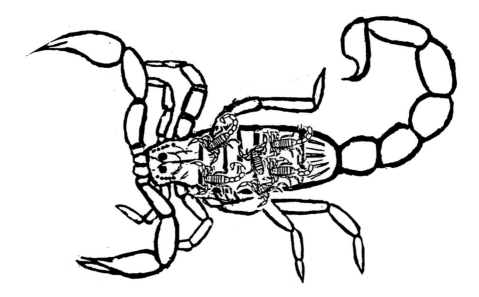

The young become solitary. They catch their own prey. They grow slowly. Some scorpions take five years to become an adult. My friend, the scorpion is an interesting desert animal.

There's Gilroy. Hi, Gilroy. What are you doing? Hi, Roscoe. I just moved this rock looking for insects. Look what I found on the underside of this rock. These are Sow Bugs. The animal has several other names, too, like Pill Bug and Wood Lice.

These Sow Bugs are relatives of shrimp, water animals. However, these are adapted to their life on land. They are found in many different habitats from the Arctic Circle to the equator. Sow Bugs are also seen in our desert under stones and desert debris.

Notice the Sow Bug has a rounded back. The back structure has a hard smooth surface.

The animal can  roll into a ball. The antennae and legs are then drawn close to the body. The  hard  cover  protects these structures from predators.

When predators, such as spiders, attack this animal, the Sow Bug discharges a sticky,  foul smelling liquid. This can discourage many a predator!

The Sow Bug has gill-like structures for breathing.

The first pair of legs is short.  These are not walking legs.  They are used for grasping food.  Sow Bugs feed on decaying plant material. They recycle this material into animal tissue within the Sow Bug's body.

The eyes of the Sow Bugs are not on stalks. Their relatives, the shrimp have eyes located on stalks.
The young Sow Bugs develop in brood pouches on the adult.  These Sow Bugs become food for many other small animals. Let's put this rock back over these  Sow Bugs.
Goodbye, Gilroy. We must be on our way.
Goodbye, Ranger Roscoe and friend.

# CHAPTER FOUR

## THE COYOTE AND THE KATYDID

**Look over there, my Friend.  That animal is a coyote.**

Photo by Earle Robinson

The coyote is larger than a fox.  It is slender and smaller than a wolf.  A coyote weighs between twenty and thirty pounds.  The coyote looks like a medium sized dog.  Unlike a dog, the coyote has a pointed nose and a bushy tail.  It also has ears that come to a point.  The coyote runs like a dog.  The tail is held downward between the hind legs of the animal when it moves.  It has slender legs.  The legs end in well developed toe pads.  It has five toes on the front legs.  There are only four toes on the hind legs.  The claws on the toes do not retract.

The coyote establishes its territory. This territory includes an area with a den and paths. The den is usually an abandoned badger or rabbit den. The coyote enlarges these abandoned dens. It can also dig out a new den.

It establishes its paths. Some will lead to water areas. Others will lead to food areas. The coyote avoids making these paths in rocky areas. Traveling on rocks is hard on the coyote's paws. It prefers paths in sandy areas and in washes. Where the paths intersect, the coyote deposits scat-feces. The territory areas are also marked with urine. In addition, at night the coyote indicates its territory by sound.

The coyote barks and yelps. This is followed by a long howl. The howl is higher pitched and shorter in duration than the wolf's howl. The howl indicates the position of the coyote to other animals. The howl also Indicates its territory to other animals.

The coyote can often be seen during dawn and dusk hours. It hunts mainly at night. It trots slowly along its path around desert plants looking for food. Mice, Kangaroo Rats, insects, and other small desert animals serve as animal food. Coyotes will also eat seeds, leaves, and fruits of desert plants.

If a coyote sees a small animal, it stops. Then it springs forward on the prey. Its paws hold down a small animal. It grabs the animal with its mouth. The coyote's teeth crush and tear the prey animal. When eating an animal, it will defend its kill from other predators. It bears its teeth, lays back its ears, and will thrust forward its front feet. This will discourage many a predator. It will leave the coyote and its food alone.

That coyote has seen us, my Friend. There it goes. It is trotting off to look for food in its territory.

My friend, look at the insect over there on that cactus. It is a Katydid. Notice. It is green in color. It blends in well on a green plant. Birds and other animals often do not notice the Katydid because of its green color.

Katydids have two pair of wings. The wings you see on that Katydid cover it like a tent. The second pair of wings lies under the "tent" wing pair.

Female Katydids have a sword-like structure on their posterior. This Katydid structure is used in depositing its eggs. The female deposits oval, flattened eggs on twigs or leaves of a plant. If it lays eggs on a twig surface, the female first roughs up the twig's surface with its jaws. Then it lays the first egg. With its sword-like structure it places the second egg a short distance underneath the lower edge of the first egg.

This process is repeated many times. Twenty of thirty eggs can be laid in a row on a plant stem. The eggs overlap one another like shingles on a roof.

The same procedure is followed laying eggs on a leaf.

Katydid eggs survive the cold winter weather. In the spring an egg splits along the top side. Out comes a Katydid! It does not have wings. It will now eat plant leaves and grow.

As the Katydid grows, new skin will be made. The old skin will be discarded. The new skin will be larger. The Katydid will eat plant food and fill out this larger skin. This happens a number of times as it grows to a mature Katydid. In these immature stages, the Katydid has no wings. It will slowly grow wings. It will set up its territory. It sings to mark its territory and also to advertize for a mate.

Katydids and crickets rub their wings together to produce musical sounds. They do this at night. A sharp edge on the front wing rubs over a file-like structure on the underside of the other front wing. This causes a wing vibration which produces the musical sounds. As fall approaches, the females lay their eggs. Cold weather will kill all adult Katydids. Only the eggs will survive the cold winter. OH, LOOK! See those two lizards on that large rock! They are Collarded lizards!

Photo by Earle A. Robinson

Collard lizards are large lizards. They range from eight to fourteen inches long. One can recognize them easily. They have two black collars across the back of the neck. These lizards are active in the morning. One can often find them on large rocks, basking in the sun. They jump from rock to rock, searching for food. They feed on insects and other lizards. At times they eat berries, leaves, and flowers.

They run after prey with their forelimbs off the surface and tail raised. If confronted by a predator, they take off running in the opposite direction.

Look, there is a large lizard over there!

*Photo by Earle A.Robinson*

# CHAPTER FIVE

# THE THRASHER AND THE CORAL SNAKE

Look! Abner is over there by that cactus. Hi, Abner! Hi, Roscoe and friend. Look at this bird sitting on its nest. All of the young are underneath it except one. Its mouth is open. It wants some food.

Photo by Earle A. Robinson

That bird is a Thrasher. It is a close relative of our Mocking Bird and the Catbird. All these birds mimic calls of other birds.

One might hear the Thrasher singing during dawn or dusk hours. It is active during the day. The Thrasher travels on the ground. It goes from one clump of plants to another clump, looking for food. It seeks insects, especially beetles, ants, and caterpillars.

The Thrasher has a long, sickle shaped bill. This bill is used in turning over small stones and desert debris. The bill is also used in digging insects out of their burrows.

The Thrasher's nest is usually found in the center of a Cholla Cactus. The nest is constructed with small twigs and lined with fine fibers. The eggs are blue-green in color, with brown speckles. The Thrasher may have two or three broods of chicks each year.

Well, I must be going, Ranger Roscoe.
Thanks, Abner, for telling us about our Thrasher.
Goodbye, Abner.

Look! There is Creosote Charley! He sees us.
Hi, Ranger Roscoe! Come over here and look at this
snake. It's a Coral Snake. As you can observe, it's a
small snake. It's just a foot or so long.

Notice. It
has a short,
flat,black head.
The eyes are
small.The body
has the shape
of a long
cylinder. The
snake is
brightly
colored.
There are black
and red colored
bands, or rings,
on the body.
In between these
bands, one can
see  narrow
yellow rings.

Photo by Arizona Game and Fish Dept.

The snake has a short tail.

One rarely sees this snake. After a rain in the fall or spring, you might find one. They emerge at night from underground or from under desert debris. The Coral Snake comes out looking for food. It feeds on lizards and other snakes.

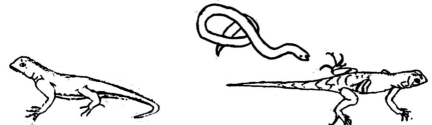

The snake grabs a prey in its powerful jaws. The muscles around a gland on each side of the upper jaw now contract. This forces poison out of the gland into a duct. Poison flows from the duct into the hollow fang. It exits out of an opening at the end of the fang into the wound of the prey. The snake holds onto the animal until it is dead. Then it will swallow the animal, head first.

When confronted by a predator, the Coral Snake buries its head in its coiled body. The underside of the tail is now visible.A popping sound comes from this posterior opening. Thanks for telling us about this snake, Creosote Charlie. We must be on our way. Goodbye! Goodbye, Ranger Roscoe and Friend!

# CHAPTER SIX

## THE BARREL CACTUS AND THE KIT FOX

There's Cactus Pete. Hi, Cactus Pete! Hi, Ranger Roscoe and Friend! Come over here and look at the orange flowers on this cactus.

Let me tell you about this cactus. This cactus is shaped like a barrel. It has a rather massive, round, columnar shape. That led to its common name "Barrel Cactus." Some of these cacti can grow over six feet high.

Holding that cactus upright are some twenty to twenty-eight ribs.  The ribs are strong "woodlike" structures.  These ribs are arranged in a circle inside the cactus ridges.

RIBS

 Looking at a cactus one can count the cactus ridges. There will be twenty or more ridges. A rib will be inside each ridge.  See this Barrel Cactus over here.  It has died and only this remains.  All the watery liquid that was stored in the center space is gone.  What is left is the thick skin covering the ridges with their ribs and areas between  ridges.

The crown of a Barrel Cactus is a major area for upward growth. New cactus takes place in this top area. This is a very sensitive area. It cannot stand the hot rays of the sun. As you can see from that cactus the crown area is completely covered by many spines.

The spines cast a shadow on the top. There are so many spines, they shield the crown area from all the sun's hot rays. So, even when the sun shines directly on it, the crown area is in the shade, which is provided by those spines.

Areoles are located only on the ridges of a Barrel Cactus. There are no areoles in the depression between adjacent ridges. The bottom bud in all areoles makes spines.

In the Barrell Cactus the bottom bud makes a large, flat, sharply hooked spine about two inches long. This is surrounded by slender hair-like spines. This central spine of the Barrel Cactus has the shape of a fish hook. This fish hook spine of the Barrel Cactus led to another common name - "Fish Hook" Barrel Cactus.

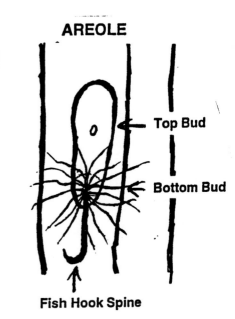

AREOLE

Top Bud

Bottom Bud

Fish Hook Spine

The top bud of the areoles in the crown can produce flowers. All flowers of a Barrel Cactus are produced only from buds in the crown area. Once the flowers have been pollinated, the cactus makes barrel shaped fruit with seeds inside. One can see the barrel shaped fruit in that cactus over there. One can also clearly see the spine produced by the bottom bud of an areole on a ridge. When mature, the fruit and seeds are eaten by many animals, such as rodents, deer, and woodpeckers.

Green plants grow toward the sunlight. In the Barrel Cactus the cells on the shady side grow slightly taller than the cells on the sunny side. This causes the plant to bend a little toward the sunny side. In our desert, this makes the cactus bend toward the south. This accounts for the Barrel Cactus's other name, "Compass Cactus." It points out the southern direction to a desert traveler.

The Barrel Cactus, like the Saguaro, stores water in its "barrel."  Also, like the Saguaro, it has features such as, thick skin covered by a wax layer, that reduce water loss.  The spines, as well as thick skin, discourage many animals from eating a Barrel Cactus.

I must be going, Ranger Roscoe, but Horatio is a few yards due south. He's looking for a Kit Fox burrow.

Thanks, Cactus Pete, for telling us about this interesting cactus.  We'll try to catch up with Horatio.

There's Horatio looking at something on the ground! Hi, Ranger Roscoe and friend. I was just looking at that hole there.  It is the entrance to a Kit Fox burrow. The fox builds a dirt mound rim around each entrance. This rim keeps surface water from entering and flooding the fox's burrow.

DEN

MAIN BURROW
ABOUT EIGHT FEET LONG

The burrow can have three to four entrances. Each leads to a two-foot, steep drop to the main burrow which may extend eight feet to the den. The den is about three feet below the surface. Here is a picture of the Kit Fox that lives in that den.

Photo by George Olin

It's a small fox, about the size of a large cat. It has a slender body, short, muscular legs, and a foot-long, bushy tail. The long, bushy tail serves as a rudder, making possible quick turns. In short dashes and turns, the fox pursues and runs down a fleeing animal. The prey, once caught, is taken to the fox's den and eaten. Kangaroo Rats, Woodrats, lizards, mice and scorpions are all prey for this fox.

Notice those very large ears. They are lined with a thick coat of long hairs. When the fox digs its burrow, or enlarges another animal's burrow, these hairs keep sand from entering the fox's ear.

Those very large ears can turn in all directions, listening for any sound in the quiet desert. One ear can listen in one direction. The other ear can listen in a different direction. Faint sounds of an animal moving on the sand will be heard. Now, both ears face in the direction of this sound. The fox's ears then twitch locating more precisely the source of the sound. In addition, the odor of the prey has already been picked up from the humid night air. The fox now stalks the animal. The soles of the feet are covered with long

hairs. The fox can walk silently on the sand.

When close to the prey, the chase begins!

The fox rests in the den during the hot day.

That's our Kit Fox, Ranger Roscoe.

Thanks, Horatio, for telling us about this desert fox. Goodbye, Horatio.

# CHAPTER SEVEN

## THE VELVET ANT AND THE COTTONTAIL RABBIT

**Look at that white insect there on the ground.**

**That   is called a Thistledown Velvet Ant.
Despite this common name, it is not
an ant.  It is a wasp.**

**Here is a sketch of that
insect without those
white hairs. Notice.
It has curved
antennae.**

All ants have "elbowed" antennae. They are bent at a ninety-degree angle. This indicates that this insect is not an ant. It has curved antennae like a wasp. It is a wasp.

Velvet Ants have a body covered with densely packed long hairs. This one has white, thistledown hairs. Ants do not have a dense covering of hairs all over their bodies like this insect. So this also tells us this insect is not an ant. The Thistledown Ant is really a wasp.

That insect there on the ground is a female wasp. It has no wings. Thistledown males have wings. The males are also larger than the females. This Velvet Ant moves quickly on the hot sand. It is searching for entrances to bee and wasp burrows. It often finds openings to burrows of the Sand Wasp.

Let me tell you about an insect food chain in our desert involving this Velvet Ant. Let's start with the Sand Wasp. The Sand Wasp digs a burrow in the sand with its front legs. Some burrows go down two or three feet. The temperature down there is some ten degrees cooler than the air on the surface above.

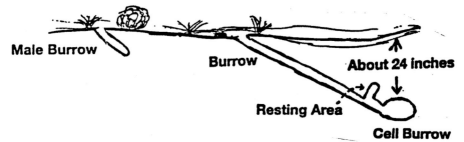

**Male Burrow**  **Burrow**  **About 24 inches**

**Resting Area**  **Cell Burrow**

The sand wasp captures flies. The poison from its stinger paralyzes each fly it captures. It carries these paralyzed flies back to its burrow.

Once there, it drags each fly down into its nest. The nest may house as many as twenty paralyzed

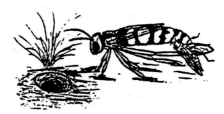

flies. The female Sand Wasp lays an egg on a fly. The egg hatches into a wormlike larva. It eats a paralyzed fly. Then it proceeds to eat other paralyzed flies. After it reaches a mature size it will change into a cocoon. From the cocoon a mature Sand Wasp will emerge. This is the life cycle of the Sand Wasp!

Now, let's go back to this Velvet Ant. It searches for these Sand Wasp nests. Finding such a burrow opening, it will enter. Down into the burrow it goes. It will lay an egg on the Sand Wasp larva. The egg will hatch into a wormlike larva. It will begin eating the Sand Wasp larva that is eating a paralyzed fly.

The mature Velvet Ant larva will then change into a cocoon. In this cocoon, the Sand Wasp larva structure it has eaten will be recycled into Thistledown Ant structures. Once completed, out will come a mature Thistledown Ant.

But the story of this food chain does not end here! The Velvet Ants, in turn, become food for other insects.

There are Bee Flies in our desert. These are large flies. The Bee Fly, like all flies, has two wings. It does not have a fly's body shape. It has the shape found in bees. Thus, it has been called a Bee Fly. It is a fly with a bee-shaped body.

The Bee Fly searches for ground burrows made by bees and wasps. This large fly's food is bees and wasps. Finding a Thistledown Ant larva or cocoon in a burrow, it lays an egg on it. The egg will hatch into a wormlike larva. This larva will proceed to eat the Thistledown Ant larva or cocoon. When mature the larva changes into a cocoon. A Bee Fly will shortly emerge from the cocoon.

The Bee Flies also attack and kill adult Velvet Ants. After killing the adult Velvet Ant, a Bee Fly feeds on its body fluids.

Those Thistledown Velvet Ants, my friend, are common in our desert. They can be found on the desert sand. One can also find them on desert flowers. They drink nectar from the flowers.

Velvet Ants will defend themselves against other wasps, ants, and even humans. They have a long stinger. Humans, stung by a Velvet Ant, find it's quite painful. Well, there goes that Velvet Ant, the wasp. However, there's much more to see in our desert. See that Desert Cottontail Rabbit!

The desert Cottontail Rabbit is smaller than the Desert Jackrabbit. These rabbits are only a foot or more long. They have large ears. They can be found in the open foothills, valleys, and plains. They establish territories in grassy and Creosote Bush areas. The Cottontails know all the dense thickets, and burrow openings in their territory.

These rabbits are short distance runners. When pursued by a predator, the rabbits will often run in circles. They know the best paths through the desert vegetation. Once ahead of a predator, they will often hide in a dense thicket or duck into the opening of another animal's burrow. The desert rabbits can be active anytime during the day. However, they are very active in late afternoon and at night. They are vegetarians. They eat fresh growth of grasses, leaves, as well as bark. In the desert these rabbits must be alert to spot predators. Coyotes, wolves, owls, hawks, and rattlesnakes all prey on these animals.

# CHAPTER EIGHT

## GILA MONSTER AND GIANT SWALLOWTAIL

There's Ebenezer. Hi, Ebenezer !
Hi, Roscoe! Come over here!
Look at this Gila Monster!
It is in this wash - this dry river bed.

That is a poisonous lizard. There are only two kinds of poisonous lizards in the world. The Gila Monster is one of these lizards. It is about twenty inches long. You can see that lizard is a very wide animal. Look at that large, fat, blunt tail.

Its skin is covered with salmon and black, bead-like structures.  This makes the skin look like Indian beadwork. Notice the banded design on the tail. See the four short, stout feet.

Those feet are ideally suited for digging out a burrow.  They resemble the feet of an alligator.

The Gila Monster is found in rocky gullies, washes, and canyon bottoms. It  is rather lethargic and moves slowly.  However, in warmer weather it does move faster. It lives in a burrow in the ground.  Sometimes it uses burrows of other animals.  It also can dig out its own burrow with those stout feet.

For nine months this lizard is inactive.  It stays in its burrow underground.  It can live for many months without eating.  The lizard lives off the fat stored in its large, wide tail.  When entering the burrow for the winter, its tail is fat and stubby.  When it comes out in the spring, its tail is much thinner. The Gila Monster has a home range. It lives in this area year after year. This territory can vary in size from four to fifty-five acres.

This lizard can usually be found in April, May, and June in our desert. During these months, it is most active. On hot afternoons, it takes a siesta in the shade or underground. It seeks food at dusk. It tends to follow a wash. Washes usually have denser vegetation. The lizard finds its food in these areas. It eats eggs, nestlings, and birds. Lizards, mice, and woodrats are also captured and eaten.

The poison glands of all snakes are located in the upper jaw of the snake. But, in the two poisonous lizards in the world, the poison glands are located in the lower jaws.

The lizard has long, pointed, grooved teeth in each jaw. Each gland has openings by the teeth. This lizard has powerful jaws. As it bites the prey, poison is secreted from the gland. The lizard slowly chews the prey. This causes the poison to move upward in the grooved, front surface of each tooth. Once inside the wound, the poison quickly kills the animal.

Sometimes the Gila Monster even turns on its back with the prey in its mouth. In this position, the poison flows downward into the wound of the prey. Once the animal is dead, the Gila Monster swallows it, head first.

At birth Gila Monsters are only about six and one half inches long. They will immediately set about seeking food. A young lizard can attain adult size in about three years. Sorry, but I must say Goodbye for now, Ranger Roscoe and friend. Goodbye, Ebenezer. We have learned much about the Gila Monster from you.

My friend, look at that butterfly over there!

That is the largest butterfly in North America. It is the Giant Swallowtail. It can be found in the eastern part of our country and up into Canada. As you can see, we also have it here in the desert. Oh, look, it has moved to the flowers to get some nectar.

Out here it lays eggs on leaves of citrus trees. The caterpillars that emerge from the eggs eat citrus leaves. The Giant Swallow caterpillar looks like a bird dropping on a leaf. Birds looking for food, do not notice them, unless they move.

Ants and other insects do find them. However, the caterpillar will defend itself. It pops out and inflates a structure from the top of its body, near the head.

Scent glands are located in the orange colored, forked end of this structure. The caterpillar sprays an acid, foul smelling, liquid on the animal.

This scent drives most animals away. All of the different Swallowtail caterpillars have this defensive structure.

After eating the citrus leaves, the caterpillar, reaches its mature size. It will now change into a chrysalis.

The tail portion of the caterpillar secretes glue-like material that attaches its bottom to a plant stem. The caterpillar then attaches a silk thread to the stem. This thread then goes around the middle of the caterpillar like a girdle. Now the caterpillar is attached to, and supported by, the stem. While this is taking place, the caterpillar changes into a chrysalis.

In this chrysalis the building blocks of the caterpillar come apart from one another. They are then reassembled in a different way. The blueprint for this new construction calls for a Giant Swallowtail. This process takes some time but eventually the change is completed. Then the casing, which houses this butterfly, splits lengthwise. The butterfly climbs out. Its wings are crumpled. It pumps liquid into the veins of the wings. This extends the wings completely. After a brief time the wing structures harden and become firm. Now the butterfly can take to the air.

That, my Friend, is the life cycle of the Giant Swallowtail Butterfly. Now, let me show you a very interesting plant, the Desert Inky Cap Mushroom.

The Desert Inky Cap Mushroom is often found after it rains. When mature this mushroom has an oval to round shaped cap. As you can see, it is white in color.

The cap's cover is not smooth. It is scaly in appearance. The cap is held up by a rather strong stalk. This is also white and scaly. The mushroom produces spores. The spores, when mature, are released and drop to the ground. Given a rain making the soil wet, a spore develops into a small fungus strand. This strand will break down small plant or animal materials in and on the soil. The fungus digests this food. It recycles plant and animal debris into a mushroom. When mature, it will be like the Inky Cap mushroom which you see there, my friend. Well, let's be on our way as there are many more interesting things to see in our desert, my Friend.

# CHAPTER NINE
## JOJOBA AND HARRIS HAWK

There's Percy.  Hi, Percy!
Hi, Ranger Roscoe and Friend!
I have been looking at that
shrub. It is tall, about six feet.
Notice, it has branches that

arise near the ground. That is a Jojoba plant.

These shrubs are found in our desert at elevations
of one to five thousand feet. The plant there is on a
sandy slope.  The Jojoba plant is an evergreen.
One finds green leaves on it all year.

The shrubs are often found in dry washes of the desert. The Jojoba plant belongs to the Boxwood family of plants. Like all Boxwood family plants, the Jojoba has leathery leaves. These are arranged opposite one another  on the stem. No Jojoba has both male and female flowers on the same bush. Female flowers will be on one bush. The male flowers will be on another bush. None of these flowers have petals.

One wonders how this plant can maintain these large leaves all year, given the hot desert sun. Most desert plants have small leaves. Take the Creosote bush, for example. It is a plant of about the same size. It has very small leaves.

The Jojoba leaf has a structural skeleton inside the leaf. This skeleton gives the leaf its shape. Most plant leaves contain a large amount of water. The water content assures the characteristic leaf shape. Thus, when a leaf loses water, it collapses, it wilts. The Jojoba leaves do not wilt even though they lack some water. The leaf shape is maintained due to this firm skeleton inside the leaf.

There is another feature that makes possible maintaining the large Jojoba leaves all year. A Jojoba leaf blade is attached to the stem by a stalk. This stalk orients the leaf blade so that the full blade faces the sun during the cooler times in a day. During the early morning and late afternoons, these surfaces receive the sunlight.
The openings in the leaf's surface allow air in and out of the leaf. Since the air outside the leaf is cooler, less plant moisture is lost through this air movement. The plant carries on photosynthesis. It makes more Jojoba plant.

When the air and leaf become hotter, the leaf openings close. The leaf shuts down photosynthesis operations. The leaf stalk now changes the way the leaf blade faces the sun's rays. Now the edges of the leaf's blade face the direct sun's rays. Less area of the leaf blade is absorbing heat from the sun. This will keep the plant cooler.

Here is a picture showing flowers on a male Jojoba shrub. The flower stem arises from the leaf axil. That is, it grows out from the stem in front of the attached leaf. Male flowers form further down on the male plant stem. When mature, these male flowers will produce much yellow pollen. Notice the male flowers do not have  showy petals.

Here is a picture of a flower on the female plant. It also hangs down from a flower stem. Green sepals enclose the lower part of the flower. One can see three flower parts projecting from the top. These receive pollen from  the yellow male flowers. Once a flower has been pollinated, it can produce a fruit containing seeds.

As the fruit matures, its shape resembles an acorn. At maturity, it is a brown-tan in color. Mature Jojoba seeds have a high oily content. The oil part of the seed might be as much as half the weight of the entire seed.

Jojoba fruits serve as food for many desert animals. Mice, rats, deer and Bighorn Sheep all eat the Jojoba fruits.

Thanks, Percy for telling us about this desert plant. Well, we must be on our way now. Good bye, Percy. Goodbye, Ranger Roscoe and Friend.

Look at that Harris  Hawk., my friend. Notice, it is dark colored. However, it has chestnut colored thighs, shoulder patches, and a white rump. There is a white band of feathers on the tail. The feather colors are the same for

Photo by Earl  A. Robinson

the male and  the female.The female hawk is larger than the male. The male is perched on that Saguaro looking for food. The nest is just up ahead,my Friend.

There it is in that Saguaro. Look! The female and two chicks are on the nest. The chicks are just losing their white, downy feathers. Let me tell you more about these hawks. The hawks construct the nest

Photo by Earl A. Robinson

with twigs. The inside of the nest is lined with grass. The female lays two to four white eggs, speckled with brown. The female incubates the eggs.

When the eggs hatch, the female stays on the nest and broods the young.  The male continues to supply the female and the chicks with food.

While the female cares for the young on the nest, the male hunts for food.  The male takes to the air, gliding slowly while scanning the desert areas below for food.  Quail, rabbits, snakes, and lizards all serve as food for these hawks.  The hawk has very fine vision.  Once it spots an animal, it dives down to capture it.  Hawks can kill

their prey by hitting it with their closed talons.  They can also kill an animal they capture by clutching it tightly in their talons.  The foot muscles drive these talons into the animal.  After catching the animal, the male will take it back to the nest.  On the nest, the hawk stands on the prey and, with its beak, will rip open the prey.  Piece by piece, the animal is taken apart and eaten by the adults or fed to the chicks.  The hawks will take good care of their chicks.

These Harris Hawks, my Friend, are carnivores. They eat animals. For example, the hawk would capture and eat a rabbit. The rabbit becomes food for the hawk. What was the food that the rabbit ate? Well, the rabbit is a herbivore. It only eats plants. The rabbit eats grass, leaves, stems, bark, that is plant structures. So our food chain now involves plants. The Hawk also eats snakes, lizards, quail, and birds. Here are some of these food chains.

| SNAKES | LIZARDS | QUAIL | BIRDS |
|--------|---------|-------|-------|
| : | : | : | : |
| MICE | INSECTS | PLANTS | INSECTS |
| : | : | | : |
| PLANTS | PLANTS | | PLANTS |

All food chains in the world start with plants. Plants take in water and air. Using energy from sunlight, the green material in plants combines water and carbon dioxide from the air. The building blocks made by this process are used in making plant structures. Roots, leaves, stems, bark, flowers, seeds, are all plant structures which are made. Plants, through photosynthesis, produce plant structures. All food chains start with plants.

Well, lets be on our way, my Friend.

# CHAPTER TEN
## THE PECCARY AND THE CENTIPEDE

Look at that wild pig, my Friend. It is one of the larger desert animals. The common name of that animal is Peccary. Another

Photo by Earle A. Robinson

common name is Javelina. This animal is about three feet long. Its body is less than two feet high. It is a rather stocky animal. The body is compressed from side to side. Notice, the head is very large. The pig has a short neck.

The Peccary has short legs. It moves fast when it runs. It does not bend its legs when it runs. It runs straight- legged. The legs end in hoofs. The body weight rests on the tips of two toes in each leg.

The Peccary's front legs have two additional toes on the sides of each leg. The hind legs have only one additional toe on the inside of each leg.

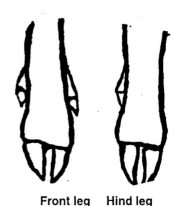

Front leg    Hind leg

About six inches forward from the tail on the back is a nipple. The nipple has an opening for the musk gland. When sensing danger, the Peccary sprays musk out from this nipple. Musk is composed of oil and perspiration. It has a rather foul odor.

The Peccary is covered by hair-like wiry bristles. Along the back, these hairs are longer. They form a mane. When frightened, these hairs are erected. This makes the Peccary appear much larger to the predator. The desert heat and wind have a drying effect on animals. This layer of hairs helps keep the animal from drying out.

In winter, the Peccary has a coarse, dark coat of hair. This helps the animal cope with winter weather. Some hairs are white in winter and form a white collar. As summer nears, the dark tips of the bristles break off. Now the hair is shorter. It is also paler in color. This adaptation helps the animal cope with summer heat. The hair of the Peccaries is very unusual. A hair bristle has radiating ribs. In between these ribs is a sponge-like tissue. No other animal has such a hair structure.

Peccaries have a long, strong snout. Lengthening the snout improves the air circulation. This makes for a fine ability to pick up odors. The Peccary can pick up odors of a predator which is still a distance away. This is very helpful since the Peccary has poor vision. The snout is also used in rooting out food, such as moist roots.

Peccaries set up territories. Their habitats are usually Mesquite or Cholla thickets. The clumps of plants provide protection from predators. The animals establish a network of trails. Some trails lead to water areas. Others lead to feeding areas. Peccaries dart in and out around desert plants in their territory. They actively defend their territories. They mark the area with musk. The animal rubs its back against low branches of trees and plants, spraying musk on these structures.

The animals usually travel in groups. Peccaries bed down in dense, shaded areas. In summmer their body heat is thus transferred to the cooler ground. This cools the animal in summertime.

In winter, the animals huddle together. This close contact keeps them warm. They do the opposite in the summer. They bed down singly, not against one another. If a predator confronts a group of Peccaries, they form a circle. The heads of the animals in the group all face outward. If a predator approaches too close, the circle explodes. Peccaries dash out in all directions.

Peccaries are mostly herbivores. They eat plants. Prickly Pear pads, Agaves, Barrel Cactus fruits, grasses and seeds are their main plant foods. When eating Prickly Pear pads, the spines are crushed by their teeth. See, part of this pad has been eaten!

They can also knock the pads down on the ground. Their hoofs then crush these pads. They secure water from the pads. Peccaries also dig out and eat the moist roots of some desert plants. This also gives them some water. Peccaries looking for food can tear apart a Pack Rat nest. They eat the stored seeds in the rat's nest.

In eating grasses, a Peccary does not use its tongue. It grabs the grass with its mouth.

Peccaries have a small mouth. It is located on the underside of the head. Peccaries chew food in an up and down motion. The canine teeth in the upper and lower jaws do not allow for sidewise action. The front edges of the upper canines shear or grind against the lower canines in eating. A bite by a Peccary can be very dangerous.

Peccaries search for food in the morning and late afternoon in the winter. In summer, they seek food early in the morning. They rest in the shade during the daytime.

Predators of Peccaries include the Puma, Jaguar, Bobcat, and Coyote.

Look at that animal on the Prickly Pear Cactus. That is the Desert Centipede. Desert Centipedes are rather large animals. Its body can be twelve inches long. All centipedes are divided into sections called segments. These body segments are flattened. The segments have hairs. These hairs are sensitive to touch. Each segment has a pair of legs. Many segments make many legs. This led to the name for these animals. "centi" means hundred and "pede" refers to legs. So, centipedes are commonly called "Hundred-Leggers".

A centipede has two eyes. These help in finding food. Two antennae are located on the head. These antennae are sensitive to vibrations. Behind the head, on the underside of the animal, is the mouth. A clawed fang is located on the first segment.

Each fang is connected by a duct to a poison gland. A muscle around the gland forces poison out into a duct. The duct ends in a fang opening. The fang

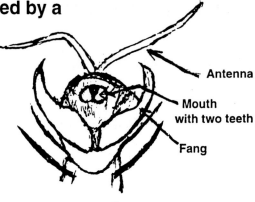

Antenna

Mouth
with two teeth

Fang

pierces the body of an animal. Poison is forced through the fang into the wound. The poison kills the prey.

Then strong toothed structures near the mouth area grasp the prey. These break up the prey into smaller pieces which are swallowed.

Centipedes hide out during the day. They hunt for food at night. Earthworms, insects, and small animals serve as food. Centipedes even eat other centipedes.

Look over there. It's Gilroy looking at something on the ground. It must be an insect.
He always finds unusual insects in our desert.

Oh, Hello, Gilroy. What are you looking at today?
Hi, Roscoe and friend. Come and look at this Darkling Beetle. Notice how it walks. Its head is near the ground. Its other end is raised up at almost a forty-five degree angle.

Photo by Arizona Game and Fish Dept.

Those hind legs are spread outwards to the ground. We disturbed it. It has stopped walking. Now it stands there rather stiffly.

An animal might try to grab this beetle for food. If it did, it is in for a real surprise. This beetle shoots out a foul smelling, black liquid from its rear end.

Many a predator, after experiencing this, will move on and leave it alone. During the hot part of most days, this beetle will rest in its burrow. It can also hide out under desert debris.

The larvae and adults of this beetle are scavengers. Plant and animal parts such as leaves, bark, flowers, and hairs on the desert floor, are eaten and recycled by this insect into a Darkling Beetle. Plant and animal debris could pile up over all living desert life if there were no scavengers. These plant and animal scavengers recycle used parts into new living structures. The Darkling Beetle is one of our many desert scavengers. It is an interesting desert insect.

# CHAPTER ELEVEN
# THE KANGAROO RAT AND TARANTULA SPIDER

**Look at that animal, my Friend.**

Photo by George Olin

**That is a Kangaroo Rat. There are many different kinds of Kangaroo Rats. All of them are very small animals. The head and body of that rat is only about five inches long. Notice. The animal does not have a neck. The head is attached directly to the body. The tail is very long, between seven to nine inches long. It is longer than the rest of the animal.**

All Kangaroo Rats hop on their hind feet like a Kangaroo. Their front feet are not used in locomotion. The rat uses the front feet like hands.

The Kangaroo Rats are great jumpers. With their powerful hind legs they can make long jumps. When chased by a Kit Fox, or Coyote, they can travel twenty feet per second in two-foot hops. When excited, the animal pounds the sand with its powerful hind feet.

To drive away a predator, those hind legs kick sand at a predator. This temporarily blinds the predator, or drives

it away. The soles of the feet are covered with long, stiff  hairs. This gives the animal good traction on the sand.

The rat's long tail acts
as a rudder when the rat
moves.  If the long tail
swings to the left, the
rat takes off to the right.

If the tail swings to
the right, the rat
takes off to the left.
These quick turns can even
take place in the air during
a jump.

The rats construct a burrow in the sand with an
entrance and den. Some construct a network of
entrances and burrows which
lead to a den. The den of some
rats might be under a three
foot deep pile of dirt and
desert debris.  This
mound can be as much as

ten feet in diameter.  There can be up to twelve
entrances to the burrow network leading to its den.

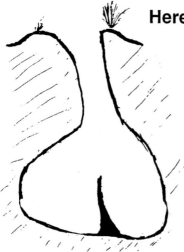

Here is a rat's burrow that ends in the rat's den and a seed storage area. The rat makes a mound of dirt around the rim of the entrance to its burrow. This keeps the den from flooding during the monsoon rains.

The Kangaroo Rat's main food consists of seeds of desert plants. When seeds are available, the Kangaroo Rat is out harvesting them. The rat picks up seeds with its front feet. The animals have cheek pouches. The pouches, one on each side, open into the mouth area. The pouches are lined with fur. The front feet put the seeds into pouches. When the pouches are full

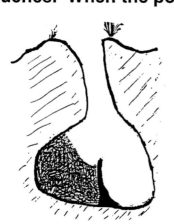

with seeds, the rat heads for its burrow. Down it goes into the den. Here the front feet empty out the seeds from the pouches. They are placed in a pile in the storage area of the den.

The rats also store seeds in other underground places. At times, some stored seeds are not needed and are forgotten by the rat. Given a good rain, many seeds will germinate. Now, there are clumps of these plants in new spots. The rat has helped distribute plants into new areas.

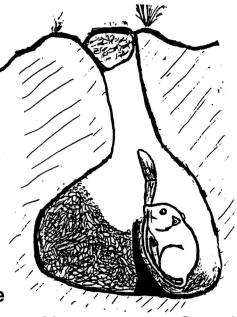

During the day the Kangaroo Rat sleeps in its cool den several feet below the desert surface. Before it sleeps, it closes off the entrance to its burrow with a plug of dirt. The rat is now enclosed in its den and burrow. The breath of the rat keeps the air in the den and burrow moist. Stored seeds are dampened. As the rat breathes, the moisture is not lost. The rat doesn't drink water. It chemically makes water from the seeds. It does nibble at times on desert plants.

This is a remarkable animal. Kit Fox, owls, and many other animals capture Kangaroo Rats for food. The Kangaroo Rat is sixty-five percent water so it is an excellent food for a desert animal.

**Look, my Friend. There is a Tarantula Spider.**

*Photo by George Olin*

Tarantula spiders belong to a large group called Wolf Spiders. These spiders are ground spiders. Wolf Spiders do not spin a web to catch their food. Rather, they wait for their prey to come by. At times, they actively hunt on the ground for food.

That Tarantula Spider lives underground. It digs a burrow in the soil. It shoots out a silk thread and lines the burrow with this silk. Burrows open above at ground level. Burrows can be under shrubs, among rocks, or under desert debris.

In late afternoon, the spider emerges from its burrow. It starts looking for food. Beetles form a major part of this spider's food. Tarantulas also capture other insects and small animals. Here is a drawing which shows the outline of this spider's body. The Tarantula, like all spiders, has two parts to its body. Four pairs of walking legs come off the front part. Notice, the long structure in front of the first walking legs. The spiders's fang lies in a groove in this structure. The sides of the groove are lined with teeth. When a Tarantula catches its prey, it erects the fang. It strikes the prey with the fangs, making wounds in its body. The muscles around the spider's poison glands contract. This squeezes poison through the poison tubes, the hollow fangs, and out the openings, into the prey. This poison starts digesting prey structures.

The spider then mashes the prey with strong, grooved teeth.  Next, it shoots digestive juices into this area.  The flesh of the prey is thus digested and reduced to a liquid.  The spider then puts its open mouth against the wound in the animal.  It sucks out the liquefied food.  All spiders eat only liquid food.  The Tarantula also uses this poison injecting fang to defend itself against other animals.

Here is a large insect, a wasp.  It is called the Tarantula Hawk Wasp! This wasp lives in the desert. Notice its black and orange colored wings.

*Photo by George Olin*

This is one of the largest wasps in our country. It is a solitary wasp. One never finds groups of this wasp. It finds and captures Tarantula Spider food for its young. The female Tarantula Wasp seeks out and attacks a Tarantula Spider. In a fight, the spider usually loses. The wasp plunges its stinger into the spider's body. A muscle contracts around the poison gland.

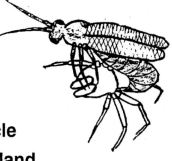

Poison passes through the stinger into the spider. This poison paralyses the spider. The spider remains alive but it cannot move. The wasp then heads for the burrow it has dug in the ground. It

drags the paralyzed spider into the burrow.

It lays an egg on the spider's body. Then the wasp comes out of the burrow. It moves soil into the opening and closes off the burrow.

The egg will hatch into a small larva, a   wormlike animal.
It will feed on the living, but paralyzed spider.
Eventually, the larva will eat the entire spider.

Now mature, this larva will change into a Tarantula Hawk Wasp.

This is what takes place.  The building blocks of the larva will gradually come apart.  These building units will then slowly reassemble in a far different way. They will form a Tarantula Hawk Wasp! This is Nature's way of recycling!

The new wasp will then emerge from the burrow in the spring.  It will seek and capture Tarantula Spiders as food for its young.  Its food is  nectar from desert flowers.  One can often see a Tarantula Hawk Wasp on flowers of the milkweed plant.

There it goes, my Friend!

# CHAPTER TWELVE
## MOURNING DOVE AND IRONWOOD TREE

Look at that bird, my Friend! You have heard this bird cooing, I'm sure. The call is a mournful, melancholy sound repeated over and over. This has led to its name. It is called the Mourning Dove.

Notice. The Dove has long tail feathers. These tail feathers are longer in the male.

The Mourning Dove is found all over the United states. However, it is not present in the coniferous forests of our mountains.

Out here these doves start nesting in mid-March. The male brings the sticks to the site of the nest. The female takes the twigs and constructs the nest. It is a platform of sticks but it does the job. Here is a nesting Dove in the desert. Eggs are laid. Doves take turns incubating the eggs. The pair can nest

and raise young, two to four times a year.
You did notice the dove on its nest, didn't you?

Birds in the desert do no live in burrows. When the surface is hot, many animals retire to cool burrows. Birds have no burrows. They have to find shade. It can be a hundred fifteen degrees in the shade on hot days. The dove cannot survive at this temperature. The dove must lose this excess heat. Birds do this by panting. In panting, the bird reduces its body temperature. Doves lose water in this process. To compensate for this loss of water, the dove must drink water. It must fly to a spring or a water source every day to obtain water.

In northern parts of our country, doves migrate south in winter. Look at that large group of doves feeding on seeds at that south western golf course.

**My Friend, look at that large tree in that sandy wash.**

That is an Ironwood tree. It is an evergreen tree. The tree has a short trunk. Notice that tree has a wide spreading crown. Its foliage is dense. That tree is broader than it is high. Leaves are alternate on the stem. Short, slender spines are located on each side of a twig where the leaf comes off the stem. Purple flowers cover the tree in late spring. The flowers are in short clusters along the twigs. When flowering, the tree is visited by many bees, insects, and Humming Birds. Many desert animals eat the seeds of this tree.

# CHAPTER THIRTEEN
# LIZARDS AND THE COACHWHIP SNAKE

**Look at that lizard, my Friend.**

Photo by Earle A. Robinson

**Lizards have a long body with a long tail. They have well-developed legs. There are five clawed toes on each leg. These legs give the lizard speed in fleeing and escaping from predators.**

**Most lizards have eyelids. Lizards can close their eyes. Lizards have a single layer of teeth in the upper and lower jaw.**

The tongues of lizards vary in size and shape. Some tongues are short and thick. Others are long and thin.

Some male lizards have bright colors. The colors are used to intimidate other male lizards. The entire lizard's body is covered with scales. These are hard structures located in the inner part of the skin. The scales serve as a protective 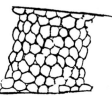 covering for the animal. Lizards shed their skin about every thirty to forty-five days. The process of shedding takes several days to a week. Skin on head, body, and tail can be shed at different times. The skin comes off in patches. The lizard rubs against objects to remove patches of skin. With the old skin off, the lizard has a new skin that is bright and shiny.

Shortly after mating, the female lays one to about twenty-five eggs. It lays these eggs in various places in its territory. The eggs will hatch later in the summer or fall.

The liquid part of the egg increases as development of the lizard progresses.
The size of the egg then can become one and one-half times the size

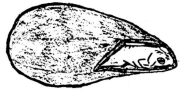

of the original egg. Each egg has an outside leathery shell. The embryo lizard develops a tooth as it nears time to emerge. The tooth grows out from the jaw. The

developing lizard soon fills the whole space inside the egg shell. This causes the sharp point of the tooth to pierce the egg shell. As the lizard's head moves back and forth, the razor sharp sides of the tooth now slice open the shell. The new lizard emerges. The egg tooth is shed shortly after birth.

Lizards live on the ground. They climb over, and on, rocks and desert debris. The number of lizards living in an area varies. In areas with many lizards, each lizard sets up its territory. The territory will include shelter areas as well as places with adequate lizard food. Other lizards entering the territory will be driven out.

Most lizards feed primarily on insects. They recognize food insects by their movements. Some lizards prey on other lizards. Lizards can "taste" their food first. They extend their tongue and place it on an insect.

If the "taste" is right, it eats the insect. If this insect doesn't "taste" good, the lizard walks away from the insect. Food other than insects is "tasted" in the same way.

Lizards, like snakes, are cold blooded animals. They lack an ability to maintain a constant body temperature. So, the lizard must derive its body heat from the desert environment. This creates a problem for the lizard. The desert is cold at night and hot during the day.

So to keep from dying, either from the cold or heat, a lizard resorts to using the sun's rays to secure and maintain a proper body temperature.

A lizard can tolerate temperatures between eighty-eight and one hundred-two degrees. A lizard, for its daily activities, needs a body temperature of about ninety-five degrees. As the desert temperature drops during dusk, the lizard's body temperature also drops. It must then retire to a warm burrow, or under a warm rock that is at least eighty-eight degrees. It rests there for the night. As day dawns, the morning sun starts to warm the desert. When the air becomes warmer, the lizard emerges and climbs onto a clump of grass or weeds. These weeds have become warmer. The clump is warmer than the nearby rocks.

Photo by Arizona Game and Fish Dept.

The lizard sits on the plants so most of its body faces the sun.

Now it basks in the warm sun's rays.  Its body temperature rises.  Meanwhile, the sun's rays have been warming the tops of large rocks.  These were too cold when the lizard climbed on the clump of weeds.  The lizard now moves over to a warm rock and hugs it.

Photo by Earle A. Robinson

It does this with most of its body facing the sun. The lizard's body receives heat from the sun's rays and the warm rock. Its body temperature rises. The sun's rays make the rock even hotter. Hugging the rock now makes the lizard's body too hot.

Photo by Earle A. Robinson

So it rises up on its legs. Now, only its feet touch the hot rock. Soon it may become too hot with the sun striking its long body. Then it faces the sun head on. This reduces the heat the lizard picks up from the sun's rays.

The lizard's body temperature will continue to rise. When it reaches ninety-five degrees, its daily activities become possible: patrolling its territory, chasing other lizards, looking for food.  Daily activities will be done at about a ninety-five degree temperature.  The lizard achieves this by moving from sunlight to shade. If it stayed in the sun, its body heat would continue to rise. Excess  heat must then be lost. Many animals have sweat glands to help reduce body heat.  The lizard has no sweat glands.  So, the lizard pants to get rid of its excess body heat.

Photo by Earle A. Robinson

It opens its mouth. Now, moisture on the tongue and mouth areas will evaporate. Much heat is needed to evaporate this moisture. Losing this heat causes the lizard's body temperature to drop. If it becomes too hot, the lizard will retire to the shade. So to maintain a good body temperature, a lizard keeps moving from sun to shade.

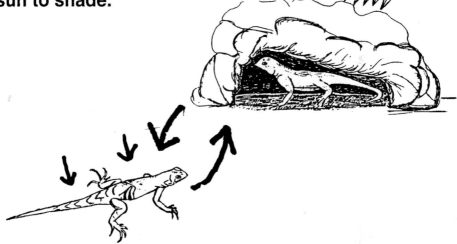

Lizards are most active in the morning. The peak of lizard activity is about ten or eleven o'clock. Lizards are again active in mid-afternoon. During late evening, night, and morning hours, the lizard remains in its shelter, a warm burrow in the ground, or, under warm rocks or desert debris. During cold or cloudy days the lizard might not come out. On the other hand, on warm nights one might find lizards moving about. Our desert lizards are interesting animals, my Friend. Well, let's be on our way.

Hi, Cresote Charlie!
Hi, Ranger Roscoe and Friend!
Come look at this snake. That is a
Coachwhip Snake. It is a large snake
with a long tail. Out here in the
Southwest, Coachwhip Snakes have
various colors, yellow, gray, brown,
and pink.

Photo by Greg Clark

**The Coachwhip can be found in our desert scrub areas during the day hunting for food.**

The Coachwhip also climbs trees looking for lizards and young birds still in the nest. It eats grasshoppers, cicadas, nestlings, lizards, snakes and rodents.

That snake moves very fast. A person chasing this snake would have to run fast just to keep up with the snake. When pursued, it might quickly climb a tree. If this tree has branches which are close to  branches of a nearby tree, the snake often moves  from branches it's on, to branches of  another tree.

When cornered, the snake coils up, vibrates its tail, and strikes repeatedly at its adversary.

The Coachwhip mates in the spring. It lays a clutch of four to sixteen eggs during the months of June and July. These eggs hatch six to eleven weeks later. The young emerging from the eggs are eleven to sixteen inches long. Well, I must be on my way. Goodbye, Ranger Roscoe and Friend.

Goodbye, Creosote Charley.

My Friend, here is a picture of a White Lined Sphinx Moth. It is securing nectar from that flower. This moth can be found in southern Canada and in the U. S. from the Atlantic to

Photo by George Olin

the Pacific. At dusk and at night, the White Lined Sphinx Moth visits the desert flowers. This is one of the animals that pollinates the Saguaro flowers. It is a strong flier with a rapid wing-beat.

This Sphinx Moth lays its eggs on leaves of weeds, tomato, tobacco, fruit trees, and many other kinds of plants. The larva stage caterpillars will feed on leaves of many plants. There are two or more generations per year. The pupae of the second group overwinter in the ground.

# CHAPTER FOURTEEN
## GAMBEL QUAIL AND DESERT MICE

There's Abner. Hi, Abner!
Hi, Ranger Roscoe and Friend!
Come and look over there.
See the Gambel Quail on
the Prickly Pear Cactus!

Photo by Earle A. Robinson

It is providing protection for many quail searching for
seeds on the ground. Let me explain this.

A male and female, with their growing chicks, join with other family groups. This is called a covey. The covey is a highly organized group. When feeding during the day, males serve as sentries. They watch out for predators.

If a predator approaches, the male sentry gives a warning call. All the birds in the covey do not move. Once the sentry notes that the predator will not pose a danger to the group it gives another call. The birds resume what they were doing - looking for seeds.

In the winter months, the quail can be observed in these coveys. However, when spring approaches this all changes. The covey organization breaks down.

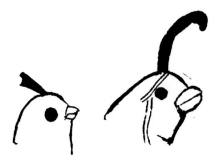

Female     Male

Male and female quail pair. After mating, the female seeks a place to lay her eggs.

A depression in the ground is selected. It is usually lined with grass, stems, and leaves. The eggs are then laid.

Here is a picture of a nest with ten eggs in it. On an average, nests usually have thirteen to seventeen eggs. The female does a good job in hiding the nest with its eggs from predators.

Photo by George Olin

The female incubates the eggs. Once the chicks emerge, the pair trains the chicks to respond to their calls. The female broods the chicks. At night, she spreads out her feathers to allow the chicks under them. The temperature control of young chicks is not too good. So, it is necessary to brood the chicks. In brooding, the chicks receive the necessary warm temperature from the female on cold nights.

In the morning, the sun warms
the ground and dries the
grass. Now, the female
and chicks head out
to feed. This occurs
shortly after daybreak.

When the chicks hatch from eggs in the spring, there
are many insects around. Most chicks begin  eating
insects. As the chicks grow older, seeds become
their major food. In the winter they often go from
eating seeds to eating greens. Just as in a covey, the
male stands guard over the hen and the chicks.

If a predator approaches, the male gives call. No one moves until the male calls again. The male also becomes aggressive to other males when it is guarding the hen and the chicks.

The family quail group seeks shelter during the heat of the day. They go out and feed again in the afternoon. After this feeding period, the hen gathers the chicks under her, providing shelter for them at night.

As summer turns into autumn, family groups combine. This forms the highly organized covey.

Cooper's Hawk

The Cooper's Hawk is the main predator of quail in the tree areas of the desert. Coyotes and other hawks also capture and feed on Gambel Quail.

Thanks for telling us about these beautiful birds, Abner. Goodbye for now. Goodbye, Ranger Roscoe and Friend. I look forward to seeing you again.

There's Horatio. Hi, Horatio!
Hi, Ranger Roscoe and Friend!
Come and look at this desert
mouse. In our desert we have
many different kinds of mice.

Pocket Mice,
Harvest Mice,
Deer Mice,
White Footed
Mice, and
Grasshopper
Mice live
here. One
finds these
mice in
areas with
dense
vegetation.

Photo by Arizona Game and Fish Dept.

As you can see, they are also found in patches of
grass and weeds. Colors of desert mice are pale gray
to brown and light brown. The mouse's color blends
in with the desert colors. As a result, predators might
not notice a mouse.

These mice have large ears, large eyes, and usually, long tails. Most mice live in burrows. Some mice dig their own burrows. Others take over burrows that other animals have made and abandoned.

Many Desert mice gather seeds when available. They store seeds in their burrows. A few mice are about during the day. These mice keep to areas with vegetation. One does not see mice out on the bare desert surface during the day. However, most mice rest in burrows during the day and seek food at night.

When days are too hot, too wet, or too cold, the mice stay in their burrows. The stored seeds are their food during those times.

In summer there are insects galore in the desert. Many desert mice eat these insects. They secure most of the water they need from insect food. Insects' bodies are about sixty to eighty-five percent water.

The Harvest Mice gather and store seeds of plants.

They store seeds in an extensive series of burrows. Seeds serve as food for these mice most of the year. However, in the spring, Harvest Mice will eat new, soft, plant growth. When summer comes, they also eat insects, especially grasshoppers.

Our desert also has Grasshopper Mice. These mice set up their territory in Creosote Bush and Mesquite Tree areas. An extensive series of burrows is constructed. The burrows provide

places to hide from predators. They also store food and raise their young in these burrows. In some desert areas, these mice breed every month. An average litter has about two to four young.

These Grasshopper mice are carnivorous. They eat other animals. Insects, especially grasshoppers, form a major part of their diet. They also eat other mice, lizards, and scorpions. They kill their prey by biting the animal on the back of the neck.

Our desert also has Pocket Mice. These are small mice. Pocket Mice are only about five to six inches long. Their tails are longer than the head and body.

The Pocket Mouse burrow is less than an inch in diameter. The burrow goes down several feet to the underground nest. One can spot these burrows. Their burrow has a mound of fine soil near the entrances. They close off branch burrows with a plug of soil.

About eighty percent of the Pocket Mouse's diet consists of seeds. During the day the mouse rests in its burrow. It hunts for food at night. It collects weed and grass seeds. These are carried back to the burrow in fur-lined cheek pouches which open into the mouth. The seeds are stored in granaries in the burrows. During hot or cold periods the mice do not look for food.

Instead the animal goes into what is called a lowered metbolic state. All body functions are reduced to a bare minimum. This state is similar to hibernation. It's like sleeping. This conserves energy. Animals, in this state, can live for a long time using very little energy.

All our mice are important in many desert food chains. They are food for Roadrunners, Hawks, Owls, Coyotes, Snakes, and other animals.

You know, Ranger Roscoe and Friend, there is another small mammal, only three to four inches long, also living here in our desert. It is <u>not</u> a mouse. It is the Desert Shrew. Here is a drawing of that animal.

The animal is covered with short, dense hair. It looks like a mouse. Notice the long, pointed snout. The eyes are very small. The Shrew can be found especially around Agave, Prickly Pear, and Sagebrush plants.

The Shrew makes a burrow which is a very small tunnel. This animal is very active. It moves about continuously looking for food. It is carnivorous, feeding mainly on larvae and adult insects. It secures enough water from the insects it consumes. It does not have to drink water.

It also eats worms, small animals, either alive or dead, fungi, and plants. The Shrew uses echolocation to find its live food. Like a bat, it sends out ultrasound waves. The sound waves strike an animal and bounce back as an echo. This echo is used by the Shrew to pinpoint not only the position of the animal but also a picture of the animal involved.

All this activity uses up a lot of energy. So the Shrew must eat twice its weight in food every day. It hunts for food for three to four hours. Then, it rests. After resting, it once again is about seeking food.

The Shrew has musk glands on either side of its body. This musk is sprayed out to repel other animals that might try to eat it.

Owls, snakes, and some mammals eat Shrews.

Well, I must be going. Goodbye, Ranger Roscoe and Friend.

Goodbye, Horatio. Thanks for telling us about the Desert Mice and the Shrew.

# CHAPTER FIFTEEN
## LADY BUG AND JOSHUA TREE

Here's Gilroy. He's looking
at a flower. Hi, Gilroy.
Hi, Ranger Roscoe
and Friend.

Look at this insect. It is called a Lady Bug. Scientists
call it a Lady Bird. It is a small insect, a beetle. Its
top pair of wings make an oval shell that covers its
head and body. Underneath these hard colored wings
is a second pair of wings. Like all beetles, the Lady
Bug can fly.

Many Lady Bugs have bright colors. Some are yellow, orange, or red beetles with black dots. Others are yellow or black with yellow or red markings. Lady Bug adults and larvae are predators. Although they eat scale insects, mites and other insects, they feed mainly on aphids, also called "Plant Lice."

Let me tell you about aphids. Here is a drawing of a winged female aphid.
Note the wings at rest are held vertical above the insect body.

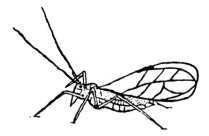

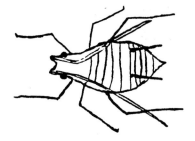

This other drawing is of a wingless aphid. Its body is soft and pear-shaped. There is a pair of upright structures at the rear of its body.

Aphids have a a bill which has an opening on its sharp, pointed end. They insert their bill into a leaf, stem, or flower of plants. Then they suck out the liquid in the plant cells.

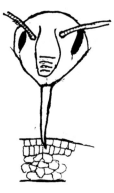

Ants tend large groups of
aphids. Aphids discharge
a clear, watery liquid
called "Honey Dew"
from their posterior.

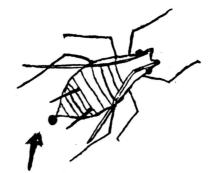

Bubble of "Honey Dew"

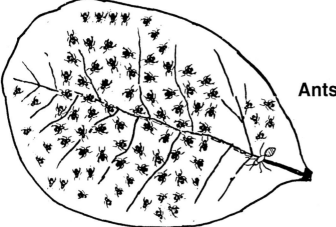

Ants regularly eat
this liquid as
they take
care of
the aphids.

Now, back to our Lady Bugs. There are male and
female Lady Bugs.
In spring, the beetles
breed. The females
lay orange colored
eggs on the
underside of leaves.
These eggs are laid in
various places near the beetle's food, the aphids.

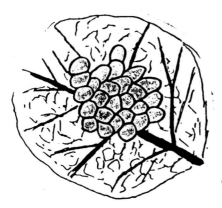

The lady Bug eggs hatch into black-colored, spiny-skinned six legged larvae.

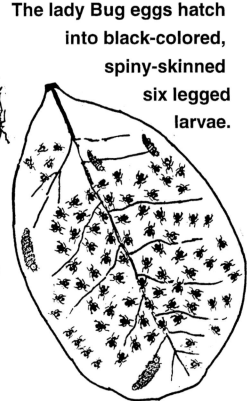

These larvae locate the aphids near by and begin eating them. After eating many aphids, a larva reaches a mature size.

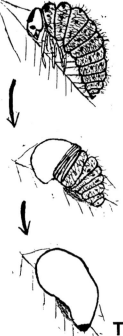

It then attaches its rear end to a leaf with a glue-like substance.

It sheds its larval skin by rolling it from its head down over its body.

The shed skin then forms a pad that adheres to the leaf. The Lady Bug is now in a pupa stage.

Building blocks of the larva now come apart. They reassemble in a far different way. The new structure that is constructed will be a mature Lady Bug Beetle. This insect overwinters as an adult.

Photo by Earle A. Robinson

Lady Bugs gather in fall in great masses on plants and under fallen leaves or bark. In freezing weather, they crawl under things to keep warm.

My Friend, look at that tree. It was named the Joshua Tree by Mormon pioneers. To them the tree looked like Joshua lifting his arms in prayer. In our Southwest, there are some thirty different kinds of Yucca plants. The Joshua tree is the largest Yucca. Sometimes it reaches a height of forty feet with a radial spread of twenty feet. Joshua trees need very hot summers and cold winters. They need a period of dormancy to stay healthy. This dormancy is brought on by near freezing temperatures for a couple of months.

The Joshua tree has long, tapering, sharp, pointed leaves with toothed margins. The tree produces waxy, white flowers in dense clusters. The leaves and flowers

are produced only in crowded clusters at the end of stout branches. The young Joshua tree normally does not branch. However, wind and insect damage to the growing top can induce branching.

Branching normally occurs if the Joshua tree has a flower cluster at the top. A Joshua tree does not bloom every year. Flowering of a tree needs certain temperature conditions and adequate rainfall. Once it flowers, growth of the trunk in that direction ceases, This seems to stimulate branching nearby during the next year.

The Joshua tree provides a home for many animals. Birds, woodrats, and some lizards can be found living in the tree. Oh, look over there at that column of leaf cutting ants.

They are carrying Creosote leaves to their underground nest. They chew up the leaves. Then they add to the leaf bits and saliva, a fungus plant. The ant larvae feed on this compost mixture.

# CHAPTER SIXTEEN
## GREAT HORNED OWL AND ASSASSIN BUG

My friend, look at that owl on the ground. That is a Great Horned Owl, the largest owl in North America.

Photo by Earle A. Robinson

Notice, the owl has yellow eyes. See the "horn" tuft of feathers on each side of the head. Those are just elongated feathers. They have nothing to do with hearing. The real ears lie behind those round discs on each side of the Owl's face.

The owl has fixed eyeballs.  They cannot be moved. We have muscles that move our eyes.  We can roll them up or down and to one side or the other.  The owl cannot do this.  Instead the owl swivels its head.

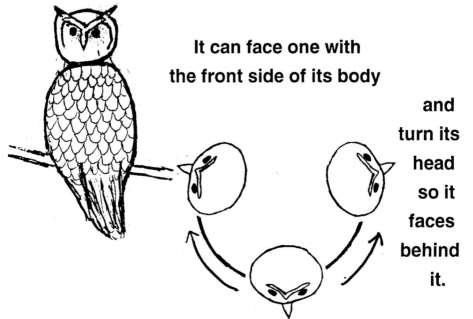

It can face one with the front side of its body and turn its head so it faces behind it.

It can swivel its head about two hundred-seventy degrees. The owl has a powerful hooked beak. The talons are covered with feathers and end in stout, curved claws.

An owl sets up its territory. It will have a nest and roosting areas.  The male calls at night to  let other owls and animals know its territory.  In spring the calls also advertize for a mate.  The calls can be heard more often during the night in springtime.

All owls lay pure white eggs. Here the Great Horned Owl laid three eggs in an old Hawk's nest. Only the female incubates nest eggs. The male hunts for food for both owls. During the day, the male owl sits in its roost. Its eyes are closed and it is motionless.

In late afternoon at dusk, the owl stretches its legs and wings. Owls hunt for prey on moonlit nights that have no wind. The male flies from a daytime perch to its hunting area. This can be quite a distance away. When hunting, the owl can fly with flight wings beating. Or, it can glide with the wings extended and beating every so often. While flying the owl's legs are pulled up against the tail.

Owls make little noise when flying. The outermost flight feathers have a comb structure. This reduces the flight sound. The soft feathers also absorb sound.

Owls capture and eat many kinds of animals. Bats, mice, rats, crows, ducks, insects, and even other owls are all food for the Great Horned Owl.

After spotting an animal the owl swoops down and seizes the body of the prey with its talons. With wings spread over the prey on the ground, the owl bites and crushes the skull with its beak. It works its claws back and forth over and into the

Photo by Earle A. Robinson

prey's body, killing it. The owl flies back to the nest. The male brings what it has captured to the female on the nest.

Sometimes the male calls the female to a nearby tree

for the food. Look, there are two young owls in that Saguaro nest. At the nest, owls hold the prey in their feet. The beak then tears apart the prey, piece by piece. These pieces are fed to the chicks.

Photo by Earle A. Robinson

All owls close their eyes when swallowing food. Surplus food is stored in the nest or in the fork of a nearby tree.

Owls cannot digest bones and hair of animals it eats. Neither can it digest chitin, the skeleton of insects. These pass through the owl unchanged. These materials come out as oval pellets. One finds these pellets below the owl's perches.

My Friend, you can learn a lot by being very observant as you walk through the desert. Just look closely at that flower there. See those insects on the flower.

The top insect is an Assassin Bug. The insect underneath the assassin is the victim.

The Assassin Bug has killed that insect and is now eating it. There are about two thousand, five hundred different kinds of Assassin Bugs in the world.

Assassin Bugs are experts in preying on and killing other insects. An Assassin Bug has a long body. It has an elongated head with stout, sucking mouthparts. Some have black and white bands on their legs.

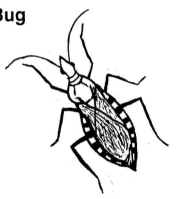

The Assassin Bugs capture insects in different ways. This bug captured the insect as it came to the flower for nectar. Powerful leg muscles grab and hold the prey. With its short, curved beak, it stabs the insect. The assassin has glands in the area behind the head that produce lethal poison. In the head is a small pump that pushes the venom into the victim through a long, strong beak that has a sharp end. This renders the insect prey helpless. Another part of this gland then produces a substance that acts as a rinsing liquid. This is pumped after the venom, through the mouth parts, diluting and cleaning the mouth parts of the poison.

These liquids now inside the insect, reduce all internal insect structures into a liquid.  A suction pump, also in the Assassin's head, now draws the liquid food out of the insect and into the digestive system of the Assassin Bug.  Soon all that is left of the victim is a hollow insect shell.

These Assassin Bugs capture insects in many different ways.  Some have adhesive pads on their legs.  These assassins run down an insect.  They grab it and hold it captive with these adhesive pads.  These pads are made up of  thousands of  hairs whose ends have a thin covering of oil.  The pads are pressed against the prey's body. The pad structure acts like a suction cup holding the prey tightly against the assassin's legs.  Then it stabs the victim and sends in venom as I have mentioned.

Some Assassin Bugs have strong bristles on their legs.  These bugs specialize in capturing  bees and hairy insects. The hairs of the insect get tangled up with the strong bristles of the Assassin Bug. The victim is captured.  Then it is stabbed and rendered helpless by the venom and eaten. Insects have to be always alert to avoid assassination!

# CHAPTER SEVENTEEN
## BURROWS AND BATS

My Friend, look at those holes in the ground underneath the Creosote bushes.

In Creosote, Mesquite, and other areas with dense vegetation, the ground can be riddled with holes like these. These holes are openings to underground animal burrows. They range in size from large to small openings. The size of the burrow entrance gives some indication of the size of the animal that made and probably lives in the burrow.

These burrows can have one or multiple entrances. The animal's den is located in the lower part of the burrow. Animals dig out their burrows. They tunnel in and around roots of trees and shrubs. Some animals take over  burrows abandoned by other animals. The burrows can be a simple tunnel or a quite complicated system of underground tunnels. Many animals could not  survive  here  in  the  desert  without  these underground burrows. The soil surface temperature in the desert  can range from very cold at night to day time temperatures that are extremely hot.

### DESERT TEMPERATUES ON HOT DAYS

Air temperature.....................103 degrees
Soil Surface temperature......155 degrees

### BURROW TEMPERATURES ON HOT DAYS

Inside temperature.................92 degrees
Two feet underground...........86 degrees

On a hot day the  burrow temperature is cooler than the temperature at the soil's surface.  In summer the temperatures on the soil surface can be about one hundred fifty degrees.  Animals cannot survive if they are  exposed to these extremely hot day temperatures.

The ground serves as a good insulator from the surface hot or cold temperature. The underground burrow temperatures are more stable. They do not vary like the extreme hot to cold temperatures on the desert surface.

So, during a hot day, many animals rest in their cool burrows. When dusk comes, these animals emerge and hunt for food. The desert is now cooler. If it becomes too cold, the animals will retire to their warmer burrows. Burrows make life in the desert possible for many animals. A burrow solves the desert temperature setup which all animals face. If it's too hot or too cold "stay in your burrow." Come out to the surface when temperatures are what the animal can tolerate.

The burrow provides other benefits to the animal. The humidity in the burrow air is higher than the humidity in the air above ground. Many animals when retiring, close off burrow entrances with a plug of soil. The animal then breathes the same moist burrow air, in and out. An animal in this burrow loses very little water from its body in breathing.

The same animal breathing dry air on the desert surface during a hot day would lose much body moisture. So most animals stay in a burrow during the day to also conserve their body water. Most burrow living animals hunt for food at night. It is cooler and the humidity in the air is higher than during the day. Again, the animal conserves its body water.

Another major burrow advantage for an animal is protection from predators. Pursued by a predator, an animal can dive into a burrow opening. Most of the time, this saves the animal's life. However, this might not always work. Some predators dig up a burrow, which the animal it is pursuing enters. Burrows that have several entrances enable an animal to make a hasty exit out another entrance while the predator digs out another part of the burrow.

However, a burrow can pose a problem if the predator is a snake. Snakes  can enter many burrows looking for food. If there is only one entrance to the surface, the animal can become snake food. Many desert animals have multiple entrances and exits to their burrow.  These animals can often exit another entrance and escape from a snake predator. Larger animals have larger burrows. Here is an entrance to a  coyote's burrow.

Burrows are also places to bear and raise young. It provides protection for the young from predators, as well as surface temperatures. Burrows are also used by many animals to store food. Ants, mice, and rats, to name a few, maintain burrow granaries of stored food.

When the desert has periods of inclement weather the animal stays in its burrow. There's no need to hunt for food. The animal eats from the food it has stored earlier in the burrow or it lives off stored fat in its body.

My Friend, there's Otis and Oswald, the twins. They work at the Vulture Gold Mine.  Hi, Otis!  Hi Oswald!

Hi, Ranger Roscoe and Friend.  We have been studying bats in the underground tunnels at the gold

mine. Bats are very interesting animals.

My Friend, bats are the only mammal that flies. Flight is made possible by a flexible wing on each side of the bat's body and a tail membrane. A large double membrane is stretched between modified hand and finger bones and attached to each side of the bat's body and hind legs.

The tail membrane is the third "wing" of a bat. It stretches between the two legs. The tail is attached to this membrane. These wings on either side and the tail "wing" make for a very efficient flight capability.

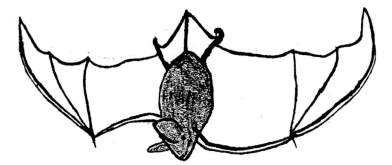

The bat's body is about the size of a mouse. The eyes are small beadlike structures. Bats' ears vary in size and shape with the different kinds of bats. Bats have long tongues used in securing nectar from flowers.

Bats do not make nests for their young. When born, the young climb onto the female and hang on for some time.

When flying on a dark night, bats avoid obstacles and find their food, which is flying  insects.

Photo by George Olin

Bats do this, not using their eyes, but by making supersonic sounds and hearing echoes from these sounds they've made. The larynx of the bat produces vocal, high-pitched notes.  These sound waves are sent out through the mouth or the nose. The sound waves strike anything in the area ahead of the bat. After striking an object  up ahead, the sounds  bounce back immediately to the bat as an echo.

From these echoes, the bat has an instant picture of what lies ahead of it, as well as its position ahead of the bat. By this means the bat finds its insect food on pitch-dark nights. This bat sonar system also helps bats avoid obstacles ahead when flying on a dark night.

This ability that bats have is echolocation. The bat analyses echoes of its own sound waves. From these echoes it receives in its ears, the bat makes a sound picture of things close by in the area ahead of it.

All bats are nocturnal animals. They are active at night. During the day they rest in trees, caves, mines, and buildings. When resting all bats hang with their heads down. The toes on their feet act as hooks holding the bat in this upside down position.

Look, my Friend, there is a Gopher Snake. It is a large snake. One has been recorded that was eight feet long. The head is small for that size snake.

Photo by Earle A. Robinson

During a hot day, the snake hides out in a burrow of a tortoise, a mammal, or under a large, warm rock. At dusk and during the night the snake hunts for food. During cool weather it also hunts during the daytime. Mice and rats are the snake's main food. However, it also eats young birds, eggs, gophers, ground squirrels and rabbits.

# CHAPTER EIGHTEEN
## TURKEY VULTURE AND PALOVERDE

My Friend, look at that large bird in the sky. It is coming our way.

I see Abner up ahead. Hi, Abner! Hi, Ranger Roscoe and Friend. Look at that Turkey Vulture. It is gliding along without flapping its wings. Now it is soaring.

Photo by Earle A. Robinson

There is a large mass of hot air rising from the ground. It supports the weight of that vulture. It makes circles inside that rising column of air.

One finds these Turkey Vultures all over North America from southern Canada down to South America. It is our most abundant vulture. It is also one of the largest North American birds of prey. It has a wing span of six feet. This vulture has a short neck, broad wings and a long tail.

The bird has a small head that is red colored. There are no feathers on the head.
It eats dead animals. With no feathers on its head , this vulture can get inside carrion without fouling its feathers. All vultures

find food by sight. The Turkey Vulture, in addition, finds food by odor. The brain area for smell in these vultures is three times the size of brain centers for odor perception in Black Vultures. Black Vultures only find carrion by sight. One often sees these vultures foraging for dead animals along roadsides.

The Turkey Vulture hunts at night. The foot of these birds is weak when compared with a hawk's foot. Hawks have strong  feet and talons for holding prey. Vultures eating dead animals do not need that strong caliber feet and talons.

The Turkey Vultures have no nests. They lay two white eggs on crevices in rocks or in a hollow tree cavity, or a hollow log on the ground. Look there are three vultures in those trees.

Photo by George Olin

These birds gather in groups to roost. Canadian and American Turkey Vultures winter in west California and southern Arizona. Well, I must be going. Goodbye, Ranger Roscoe and Friend.

Goodbye, Abner. Thanks for telling us about the Turkey Vulture. Well, my Friend, there are still many things for us to see in the desert. If you look toward that wash, you'll notice a tree in full bloom. That, my Friend, is the state tree of Arizona. It's a Paloverde tree.

Paloverde is Spanish for Green Stick. It is named Paloverde because it has green or blue-green trunk. These trees have many branches producing a wide spreading crown.  The twigs grow in a zig-zag fashion. Twigs end in short, stiff spines about two inches long. Palo Verde trees can grow to about twenty-five feet high.

From March to May the tree has compound leaves. Each leaf has five to seven pairs of leaflets. These leaflets fold together late in the afternoon.  They stay folded through the night. They unfold again at dawn.

The tree is covered with bright, yellow flowers in April and May.

Once pollinated, the flowers develop into narrow, oblong seed pods. The pods have sharp, pointed ends.

Each pod encloses from two to eight bean-shaped seeds.

During dry, hot periods the tree loses all its leaves. During these times, which are most of the year, the green bark carries on photosynthesis.

My Friend, look at that cactus. That is a Night Blooming Cereus. This cactus, has a woody stem, a gray-green stick. The stem grows up about four feet into low branches of desert trees. The ribbed stem is only about one-half inch in diameter. Other branches come off it. Flowers are produced on this stem. The white flowers last only one night. They give off a pleasant odor. Animals pollinate the flowers. At dawn the flowers will close. A pollinated flower will form an orange colored fruit, with seeds. The fruit looks like an oblong tomato.

The fruit has some spines on its outside. Inside is a red pulp with many black seeds. Birds eat the pulp. They digest the fruit, but not the seeds, which are then deposited in their droppings. The seed germinates making a small cactus plant. It is a stem that carries on photosynthesis. Early on, it makes an enlarged underground root in which it stores water. This root can range in size up to some weighing thirty pounds. The plant stem, above ground, branches into a number of side branches. All these stems have areoles,

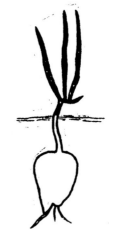

a characteristic of all cacti. The bottom bud of these areoles makes about a dozen minute blackish spines. These spines lie parallel to the stem. The top bud of the areole can make a flower. These flowers have been produced by the top bud of areoles on this stem. Water is so important in a desert. Many desert plants store water in their leaves, as in the Agaves. Some store water in their stems, as in many cacti. Some store water in underground roots, as the Night Blooming Cereus. During dry periods this plant uses water from its underground turnip-shaped tuber.

Well, my Friend, we have, for now, come to the end of our travels with you through the Sonoran Desert. We hope that you have enjoyed traveling with Ranger Roscoe. You have learned how many plants and animals live here in the desert. In our travels together, you have met interesting desert animals, the Gila Monster, Sonoran Coral Snake, Road Runner, and desert bats, just to name a few.

You have observed how many desert plants have become specialized in order to cope with life in a dry, hot desert. You have seen how many desert animals have changed their behavioral patterns to make possible living in our desert.

You have seen many of these interesting desert plants and animals. However, we have just skimmed the surface on life in the Sonoran Desert. There are still many additional animals and plants that live in our desert.

My Friend, you will have to travel with us through our desert again. We are still working on another book to complete the series of books on the Sonoran Desert.

# TRACKING IT DOWN